6.5

The Library of Author Biographies

Gary Paulsen

The Library of Author Biographies

GARY PAULSEN

Sarah L. Thomson

the rosen publishing group's
rosen
central

Published in 2003 by The Rosen Publishing Group, Inc.
29 East 21st Street, New York, NY 10010

Library of Congress Cataloging-in-Publication Data

Thomson, Sarah L.
Gary Paulsen / Sarah L. Thomson.—1st ed.
    p. cm. — (The library of author biographies)
Summary: Discusses the life, publications, and writing habits of Gary Paulsen, author of such popular novels as "Hatchet" and "Dogsong," as well as non-fiction works.
Includes bibliographical references and index.
ISBN 0-8239-3773-9 (lib. bdg.)
1. Paulsen, Gary. 2. Authors, American—20th century—Biography. [1. Paulsen, Gary. 2. Authors, American.]
I. Title. II. Series.
PS3566.A834 Z88 2002
813'.54—dc21

2002006690

Manufactured in the United States of America

Table of Contents

Introduction:
In the Wilderness

In Gary Paulsen's best-known novel, *Hatchet*, Brian—the main character— watches a man die of a heart attack, starts a fire without a match, is trampled by a moose, gets sprayed by a skunk, kills a deer with a bow and arrow, is nearly smothered by mosquitoes, and eats turtle eggs.

All of these things have happened to Gary Paulsen—except the turtle eggs. Paulsen did try to eat turtle eggs, but he couldn't manage it. He has eaten squirrel entrails, grub worms, and rabbit brains, and he has sucked the eyeballs out of fish, but he couldn't swallow a turtle egg, although he tried three times. "They hung halfway down my throat," he wrote later in an autobiography, *Guts*, "and tasted the way I imagine Vaseline would taste if, somehow, it were rotten."[1] Paulsen threw up until he had dry heaves and abandoned this attempt at research for *Hatchet*. But he left the incident in the book, believing that if he had been as hungry as Brian was—if he had been starving—he would have swallowed the eggs.

Everything else in *Hatchet*, however, is based on incidents in Gary Paulsen's own life. This is true of all his books. Paulsen is particularly well known as the author of suspenseful adventure stories, where young protagonists struggle to survive on their own in the natural world. Thirteen-year-old Brian Robeson, the main character of *Hatchet* and three other books, is stranded by a plane crash in the Canadian woods. Russel, of *Dogsong* (like *Hatchet*, a Newbery Honor book), runs a team of sled dogs through the Alaskan wilderness. David Alspeth rides out a storm at sea in *The Voyage of the Frog*.

Although to most readers Paulsen is best known for his survival stories, his other works touch on different aspects of his own adventurous and often difficult life. Events from his childhood visits with relatives on Minnesota farms are retold in such novels as *The Winter*

Room, his third Newbery Honor book, and *Harris and Me*. His relationship with his gentle, nurturing grandmother gave rise to *The Cookcamp* and *Alida's Song*. Memories of a summer when he ran away from home, hoed beets with immigrant laborers, and worked at a carnival later shaped two works, the novel *Tiltawhirl John* and a memoir, *The Beet Fields*.

Most of Paulsen's life has been lived close to the natural world—hunting, fishing, trapping, sailing, running teams of sled dogs. This has meant a life filled with danger. Often, Paulsen has been close to death and barely managed to save himself. Sometimes, when he wasn't able to save himself, he had to rely on help. That help didn't always come from other people.

In January 1980, Paulsen was running a team of sled dogs by himself along a trapline in northern Minnesota. He and his wife lived in a small cabin in the woods, and Paulsen made money by trapping beaver, for which the government paid a small fee. He stopped the sled on the ice of a frozen lake near a lodge, a construction of wood, mud, and stones, partially underwater, where beavers make their home. Paulsen knew that the ice near a lodge is usually thin, because the beavers swim underneath it, releasing air bubbles that rub against the ice and brushing it with their fur. But he didn't realize just how thin it was.

The ice broke underneath him, and Paulsen fell so quickly that he could barely react. He only had time to do two things. The first was to grab at a rope that lay across the ice, still attached to the nearby dogsled. The second was to scream. Then he was underwater, dragged down by the weight of his heavy winter clothes.

Paulsen thought he was going to die. And he would have, but his scream had alerted his lead sled dog, Cookie. She managed to get the other dogs on their feet. Together they dragged the sled away from the hole in the ice, which pulled Paulsen, still clinging to the rope, up out of the water and to safety. If it had not been for his dogs, he would have died under the ice of a frozen Minnesota lake. It was a favor he would later repay.

In the winter of 1984–1985, Paulsen was in Alaska, training for his second attempt at the Iditarod, a grueling dogsled race. He had taken his dogs on a training run and had a terrible headache; the strap on his headlamp was too tight. Distracted by the pain, he failed to notice signs—the restlessness of a dog, the wind picking up, the first few flakes of snow—that the weather was about to turn worse. Before he knew it, a blizzard had swept in. Paulsen realized this fact only when he turned a corner of the trail and was blown—dogs, sled, and all— down the face of the mountain. Luckily for Paulsen, his headlong tumble stopped near a small overhang of rock. He crawled into this shelter and discovered, to his surprise, that his sled was nearby. The snowhook, an anchor used to hold the sled in place, had caught on a crack in the rocks. With the gear on the sled, Paulsen could hope to huddle in the tiny shelter and wait out the storm.

But there was one problem with that plan: if the sled was nearby, his dogs were somewhere close as well. And they were in great danger. Paulsen could have stayed in the shelter. It was insanely risky to venture back out into the wind that had already blown him down a mountain. He might lose his footing again and tumble farther down the slope, and the odds that he would end up near shelter and his gear a second time were very slim indeed. But he couldn't accept a solution that would let him survive while his dogs perished. "I knew I couldn't allow that," he explains. "In some way we had gone past where that could be allowed, gone past where I could have lived with myself, gone into an area where it had become we, instead of I."[2] He crawled to the sled, felt his way down the rope to the dogs, untangled them from the harness, and dragged them back up the slope. They slept in the shelter together while the storm blew over.

When Paulsen crawled back out of the shelter into a sunny Alaskan morning, he saw that the snowhook by which the sled had been anchored—the hook on which his life and the dogs' lives had depended—was caught by only one claw on a tiny projection of rock. As he reached down to pick it up, the movement of his hand brushed it loose from this precarious hold. Beyond the sled, he saw a huge canyon and a vertical drop straight down to a frozen river at the bottom. The slightest mistake would have sent Paulsen and his dogs tumbling to their deaths over the edge of the cliff.

That night, Paulsen saved his dogs. He saved them because he thought of them not as pets or as working animals, who were somehow his possessions, but as a team of which he was a part. Through years of living in intimate contact with nature, Gary Paulsen had come to realize that he was not separate from his dogs, or from other animals, or from any part of the natural world. This understanding changed the way he lived—he stopped hunting and trapping animals. It changed the way he worked with the sled dogs who took him a thousand miles through the Alaskan wilderness. And it shaped the books that he wrote, where, again and again, characters like Brian Robeson of *Hatchet* find that they must not conquer the natural world, but rather become a part of it and listen to what it has to teach them. Only then can one survive.

1 Growing Up Alone

Gary Paulsen was born on May 17, 1939, in Minneapolis, Minnesota. His father, Oscar Paulsen, was an army officer stationed there when he met Gary's mother, Eunice Moen. Shortly after Gary's birth, Oscar Paulsen was called to fight in World War II. He spent most of the war in Europe. Gary was much too young to remember his father and would not see him again for seven years. Gary's mother moved with her son to Chicago, Illinois, in 1944, when Gary was four. She took a job at a munitions factory (where weapons for the war effort were built), leaving Gary in the care of a woman named Clara. Clara's "care" was not particularly thorough; she drank red wine out of jelly jars, listened to the radio, and mostly ignored the young child she was supposed to be watching.

Even when his mother was home from work, Gary was not closely supervised. One weekend while his mother was taking a nap, young Gary slipped outside to play in a nearby alley. Suddenly, he was grabbed by a man—filthy, smelling of alcohol, urine, and vomit—who lifted the terrified child up off the ground. Gary was too frightened and shocked to struggle, and he would have been molested by this man if his mother had not appeared. She attacked the man, hitting him in the head until he dropped Gary, then knocked him down and kicked him with her heavy, steel-toed work shoes until he lay still—perhaps dead.

When she saw a threat to her son, Gary's mother was savagely protective. Once, when Gary was very young and in the hospital with pneumonia, the doctors believed that he would not live. They called in a priest to give him last rites. But when Gary's mother saw the priest— who to her suggested death—she could not stand the thought that her son might die. Furious, she shouted at him and drove him from the room as if her anger would be enough to keep her child alive. She had attacked Gary's molester with the same kind of rage.

One night, Gary woke up to hear his mother crying. Gary's mother told him that she was lonely and that his father had a "friend" where he was stationed in France. Gary's mother began to come home late with alcohol on her breath, and on weekends she took the four-year-old Gary to bars with her.

Soon, Gary's mother had a "friend" of her own, a man named Casey. Casey moved in with Eunice and Gary and stayed until the end of the war. During Casey's first year with the family, Gary was sent to spend the summer with Eunice's mother, who worked as a cook for a work crew cutting a road through the Minnesota woods. The nurturing warmth of Gary's grandmother and the affection of the tough working men who adopted the little boy is retold in Paulsen's novel *The Cookcamp*. But at the end of the summer, Gary returned to the uncomfortable situation of living with his mother and "Uncle Casey."

At last, in 1945, World War II was over. Gary, now six years old, thought this meant that Casey would finally leave and his father would come home. And Casey did indeed move out, but Gary's father did not come back. Instead, he was reassigned to the Philippines.

In 1946, Gary's mother managed to get both herself and her son to San Francisco, where they were to catch a troopship to the Philippines. But along the way, Gary caught chicken pox. He would not have been able to pass the medical exam required to leave the country, but Gary's mother convinced the ship's captain to help. The seven-year-old boy was smuggled onto the ship and left alone in a cabin overnight, until his mother came on board the next morning. The ship set sail, but Gary had to stay in the dispensary, where sailors went for medical treatment. He was there for nine days. A corpsman (or medic) named Harding looked after him, bringing him food and reading comic books to him.

The first time Gary was allowed out of the cabin should have been exciting—he would see the sky for the first time in over a week and the ocean for the first time in his life. But instead, it was horrifying. As his mother brought Gary up on deck, a plane crashed into the ocean near the ship. Gary watched as the plane hit the surface and broke in half. Survivors spilled into the water and climbed out onto the wings. Some were hurt and bleeding. Gary would learn later that the people on the plane were the wives and children of soldiers coming back to the mainland of the United States from Hawaii.

Much later, when Paulsen was writing *Hatchet*, he remembered this crash, especially the jolt of the plane striking water that seemed as solid as cement because of the aircraft's speed when it hit.

Boats from the troopship set out at once to rescue the survivors, and it seemed that everything might be all right. But then sharks attacked. These sharks had been following the ship for miles, eating the garbage that was thrown overboard. They smelled the blood of the injured people and attacked the survivors who fell or jumped into the water to get away from the sinking plane. Horrified, Gary watched as people died in the water before the boats could reach them.

After the injured survivors were brought onto the troopship, Gary's mother helped the corpsman, Harding, take care of them. Several children had been on board the plane with their mothers. One, a little boy no bigger than Gary, died on the deck as Gary watched. When

Gary made his way down to the dispensary where he had been staying, he found it full of survivors needing care. Looking around for his beloved stuffed animal, Dog, Gary spotted him at last—held tightly in the arms of an injured little girl. Gary decided to let her keep the toy.

As the ship changed course and headed for Hawaii, Gary made friends with a boy named Jimmy, whose mother had been killed in the crash. Jimmy never spoke except to swear at the sharks who were still following the ship, but together he and Gary explored the troopship from top to bottom. After taking Jimmy and the other survivors back to Hawaii, the ship resumed its original course, and eventually Gary and his mother reached the Philippines. At last, when he was seven years old, Gary met his father.

Oscar Paulsen was a decorated soldier. He had worked his way up the ranks to major and had fought in Europe and Africa. Gary had often thought about what it would be like to meet him, dreaming of a father who would scoop him up in his arms, who would give him all sorts of gifts and toys. But when the time came, Gary found that he was shy, almost frightened. His father promised that they would have plenty of time to get to know one another. "And because I was young and didn't know any better," Gary Paulsen wrote later, "I believed him."[1]

2 War Zone

The Philippines had been occupied by the Japanese army during World War II and retaken by the Allies in 1945. The fighting had devastated the country. From the dock where the ship landed, Gary could see the signs of war: rubble in the streets, a building with the windows and floors blown away, and craters in the road big enough to hold a truck. And the violence was not over. There was still fighting going on between a guerrilla group and the American military. The guerrillas, called Huks, wanted the government to divide the estates of wealthy landowners among the poor.

Gary's new home was on a military compound near Manila, the capital of the Philippines. He would live there for the next three years. Unfortunately, Gary's hope of getting to know his father wasn't to be fulfilled. Oscar Paulsen was busy with work, and he rarely spoke to his son except to give orders or to tell him rules. Gary's mother was quickly caught up with the social activities of an officer's wife—playing cards, having tea parties, and going to ladies' nights at the officers' club. But there was a worse problem, one that was to take Gary's parents away from him in a deeper way. Both of them were drinking heavily. Gary rarely saw them, and when he did, they were usually drunk.

Once again, Gary was on his own. There was a school on the military base, but because there were so few children and because fighting was still going on, classes were often canceled. Gary had plenty of time to explore, and he soon became bored with the usual activities near his home: watching the monkey the neighbors kept chained up in the backyard, looking at the trucks driving by, and playing inside the rusty remains of a bombed-out Japanese tank.

There were no other children nearby, but Gary did have a companion. Rom was one of the two Filipino servants Gary's father hired to help run the household. He made time to play with Gary and found a bicycle to take him for rides around the compound. They watched planes at the airstrip and rode to the exchange (a military-run store) to buy cups of warm Coca-Cola. Rom also took him to play inside a downed Japanese airplane.

But Gary soon grew restless and wanted a wider world to explore. His father had forbidden him to go outside the military compound; he might have been kidnapped by the guerrillas. But Gary found a way to get around his father's restriction. One day, he caught Rom stealing two cans of sardines from the kitchen. There were almost no jobs in the Philippines at that time, and most people were desperately poor. Rom needed the food to feed his family. But if Gary told on him, Rom would be fired. It would be almost impossible for him to find another job. His family might starve. From that time on, Rom did anything that Gary wanted. And what Gary wanted was to go outside the compound.

During their first time outside the base, Rom saw a boy working with water buffalo in a rice paddy and arranged for Gary to ride on the buffalo's back. On later trips, they visited Rom's family in their two-room shack and ate rice and sardines with them. Gary learned to like baloots, a Filipino delicacy that consisted of duck eggs allowed to sit in hot sand until the body of the unhatched duckling inside had partially rotted. He found them especially good when washed down with warm Coca-Cola.

Gary questioned Rom about the war and the Japanese occupation. When Rom told him about a nearby cave filled with the corpses of Japanese soldiers, Gary insisted on going to see it. The entrance to the cave was blocked with dirt, but Gary saw a small hole. Before Rom could stop him, he scrambled inside. There were skeletons inside, clad in rotting uniforms. But even worse, there were rats that had grown huge from feasting on the dead bodies. Panicked, Gary screamed for Rom, who came to get him and brought him back outside into the sunlight. Rom waited patiently until Gary stopped crying. Afterward, they never spoke of the cave again.

During his first year in the Philippines, Gary found a second companion. Her name was Snowball, and she was his first dog. In the Philippines, it was common for people to eat dogs, and Snowball was destined for the cooking pot before Gary saw her and begged his mother to save her. Gary's mother bought the puppy, and Snowball and Gary became inseparable. Snowball was the first of many dogs in his life to teach Gary a new way of looking at the world, using every sense to discover as much as possible about his surroundings. "I would see things," Paulsen recalled,

> blown-apart buildings, old tanks, Jeeps upside down, rusting guns everywhere—but Snowball would know things. She would see the obvious outside way a thing looked, but then she would move to it and smell it and perhaps lick it and dig at it and look under it and I took to doing the same things.[1]

Following Snowball's lead, Gary became more aware of everything around him. Not aware enough, however, to notice a snake near his bare foot before Snowball leaped at it and killed it. Later, he would learn that this type of snake was deadly. Snowball had saved his life.

During the years that Gary spent in the Philippines with Snowball and Rom as his companions, he grew more and more detached from his parents. One of the few events he did share with his mother and father was a trip to a nearby island. Gary's father arranged a canoe trip down a river to a scenic lake. While the adults ate a picnic, Gary, who couldn't swim, played in the shallows.

Everything would have been fine, except that Gary found a log to float on and was soon washed into violent rapids where the river flowed out of the lake. He would have drowned if a young Filipino boy had not grabbed him and pulled him out of the water. Gary's mother held her son tightly, shaken at the near loss, and then pulled him back into the lake, dragging him by the hand as he struggled against her. She insisted that, if he didn't go in the water, he'd be afraid of it for the rest of his life. Fully clothed, she knelt down and played with him in the shallow water until he was no longer afraid.

This was one of the few times Gary felt connected to either of his parents. "Truthfully I didn't see them very much," he wrote, and in some ways did not want to see them. Father was a stranger, and Mother . . . was fast becoming somebody I no longer knew. They were drunk almost all the time now . . . Every night they drank and every night that they were home and drinking they fought.[2]

Snowball was a more reliable friend. Gary would talk to her about the problems in his life, and she seemed to understand. Sadly, just two weeks before Gary and his family were to return to the United States, Snowball was hit by a truck while she and Gary were walking by the side of the road. "I remember standing, not believing she was dead," Paulsen wrote much later, "thinking how nothing would ever be right again, not ever, and how I would always, always miss her, and that is all true. . . I miss her as much as if she'd died yesterday."[3]

After three years in the Philippines, in 1949, Gary and his mother returned to the United States. His father followed shortly afterward. They spent nine months in Washington, D.C., while Gary's father finished his military service at the Pentagon. Then the family moved back to Minnesota.

3 Running to the Woods

I was one of the wasted ones," Gary Paulsen wrote in a memoir about the years he spent with his family in Minnesota. "One of the emotionally injured, who awakened crying in the night, the boys who saw with wide eyes and could say nothing."[1]

Gary's parents' problems with alcohol continued. It seemed as if they did nothing but drink and fight. When the family first moved back to Minnesota, Gary's father made an attempt to raise chickens for a living. When that didn't work out, Oscar Paulsen tried his hand at other kinds of work to supplement his military pension—tending bar, managing a liquor store, and working in a gas station. But his jobs rarely lasted for long, and the family had little money.

School wasn't much better than home. Since the family was constantly moving while Gary's father tried new jobs, the longest time Gary spent in any single school was five months. In *Father Water, Mother Woods,* Paulsen remembered what school felt like:

> Trying, trying to fit in, trying to be part of, trying to understand, trying to learn, trying to be accepted, trying to look right, trying to act right, feel right, say right, do right, be right.
>
> And failing at all, most, all. Grades bad, clothes wrong, never any money, hair that never worked into a flattop or a ducktail—just impossible. To wear wrong clothes and be from the wrong place in the town and have the wrong parents and think the wrong thoughts and to feel, to suspect, to know that everyone is looking, pointing, laughing. School.[2]

From the age of thirteen or fourteen on, Gary worked as many jobs as he could, trying to earn enough for spending money and clothes for school. He sold newspapers in bars, waiting until late so that his customers would be drunk enough to pay a little more. He set pins in a bowling alley until 11:30 PM on weeknights. He spent summers working on farms, doing backbreaking labor all day long for as little as two dollars and his meals. The summer he was sixteen, Gary ran away from home for a time. He headed west, where he ended up working alongside migrant workers from Mexico, something he describes in *The Beet Fields*:

> The North Dakota sun came up late.
>
> They were already in the beet fields and had taken up their hoes with the handles cut off so they could not be leaned upon to rest; had already eaten cold beans and slices of week-old bread from the metal pie pans nailed to the table to be hosed off between shifts of eaters; had already filled themselves on rusty water from the two-handled milk cans on the wagon at the end of the field . . . Had done all of these after sleeping the short night on feed shacks in sleeping sheds near the barn; after they had come into a new day, then the sun came up. [3]

Running away from home was only one of the ways Gary tried to escape the difficulties of his life. When things got particularly bad with his parents, he would stay with his mother's relatives. He spent his eleventh summer with his mother's cousin and his family, a time that later became the basis for the novel *Harris and Me*. His experiences of farm life with his relatives helped shape his Newbery Honor novel *The Winter Room*, which is a tribute to the power of land and family, memory and storytelling:

> Every night in winter it starts the same. Uncle David and Nels will fill their lower lips [with tobacco] and Father will carve and Mother will knit and the yellow flames will make our faces burn, and then Uncle David will spit in the coffee can and run his hands on his legs and take a breath and say:
>
> "It was when I was young . . ."[4]

Sadly, the visits to relatives always ended, and Gary would have to go home. After a while, he simply moved into the basement of his family's apartment building. He found an alcove behind the furnace with an old couch and a light bulb hanging from the ceiling, and he spent most of his time there. His parents didn't notice that he had more or less moved out.

Another escape opened up unexpectedly one cold night when Gary was fourteen. He was selling newspapers, and, noticing that the library was open, he wandered in to warm up.

To his surprise, the librarian asked if he would like a library card. "So she gave me a card, with my name on it," he remembered, "and—God!—it was astonishing what happened to me. It was as though I suddenly had an identity: I was a person."[5]

It took Gary a month to read the first book the librarian found for him. When he brought it back, she gave him another. Soon he was reading two or three books a week. "It was as though I had been dying of thirst and the librarian had handed me a five-gallon bucket of water," he said. "I drank and drank."[6]

When Gary was fifteen, he met a man who helped him deal with the struggles of life with alcoholic parents. J.D. was a police officer, and Paulsen calls him "the primary reason I did not wind up in prison."[7] J.D. caught Gary trying to break into a garage. He didn't take the boy to jail or home to his parents. Instead, he drove Gary out of town and made him walk the six or seven miles back in freezing, mid-January weather while J.D. followed along in his car. When Gary was sure he wasn't going to break into any more garages, J.D. drove him to a diner for a meal.

For two years, Gary spent almost every night in J.D.'s squad car. J.D. was a tough man with little patience for people he didn't like. He was known to hit suspects he had arrested (as long as they were men; it was against J.D.'s principles to hit a woman or a child), and he took violent revenge on people he believed had insulted or injured him.

But he could also be protective, and for reasons Gary never quite understood, he saw something worthwhile in a rebellious teenager who was known to be the son of the town drunks. J.D. helped Gary learn to stand up for himself.

In the end, however, it wasn't J.D. or the librarian or his mother's relatives who did the most to help Gary survive his teenage years. The woods were Gary's best refuge. "I ran to the woods and rivers of northern Minnesota," Paulsen wrote of himself and his friends.

It was, I suppose, a kind of self-fostering— perhaps a subconscious seeking of help from nature . . . In the normal run of things our lives hurt. When we were in the woods or fishing on the rivers and lakes our lives didn't hurt.[8]

There were other boys like him who needed the money and food that hunting and fishing could bring. Gary's parents could not always be relied upon to keep the kitchen stocked with food or give him the money he needed to buy it, and when Gary didn't eat the fish and game he caught, he sold it to pay for clothes, supplies for school or hunting, or hamburgers and milkshakes. After school, on weekends, and on the days he simply chose not to go to school, Gary fished at the local dam and, with a spear or bow, in the drainage ditches—the same way Brian Robeson would catch fish in *Hatchet*. Gary and his friends hunted for grouse, deer, or rabbits. And they hunted simply to be outside, where there was beauty everywhere.

> The morning light wraps a tree, catches the ice, becomes a dance, almost light-music. Things seen every day—a limb, a leaf, stones, swamp grass—all take on a change with the morning light and it stops not just one boy but all the boys; stops all of us just inside the woods.[9]

"Hunting virtually became my life," Paulsen later wrote.[10] He had spent so much time in the woods that when he was fourteen, he was able to track a deer for two days. One night, he finally got close enough to the animal to touch it. But when he told his classmates about his achievement, hoping to impress them, no one believed him.

An uncle gave Gary his first rifle. He would pack matches, bread, salt, and an old aluminum pot, and spend his weekends in the woods. After a while, he came to prefer a bow to the rifle. Although hunting with a bow is much more of a challenge, it forced Gary to pay closer attention to his surroundings. "Hunting with a bow changes all things, even the way to move," he remembered. "You had to get close to the game—15, 20 feet (4.6 to 6.1 meters)—and to do that you had to study it, know it."[11]

Just as Brian would do in *Hatchet*, Gary made his own arrows—although Brian had to cut his own arrow shafts and Gary got his from a mail-order catalog. And like Brian, after endless practice, Gary learned to look into the absolute center of the target and send the arrow directly there. Hunting with a bow was not easy. Once Gary shot ten arrows at a grouse not ten feet (3.1 meters) away, missing every single time. The bird sat still as Gary crawled forward, hoping he could retrieve an arrow. The grouse didn't move until Gary was close enough to touch it, and then it exploded into flight, right in Gary's face.

After many attempts, Gary—like Brian would do in *Hatchet*—killed his first deer with an arrow. At first the doe hardly seemed to react, and Gary believed that he had missed her—until he saw his arrow in the grass, covered from point to feathers in blood. The doe walked a few steps away, settled down in the grass, and died. Gary knew that he "had in less than a second ended something beautiful, something that would never be again, ended this doe . . . Her world . . . I have ended her world."[12]

It was something he never forgot.

4 A Ruined Life

Despite his struggles in high school (including flunking ninth grade), Paulsen eventually graduated. He was accepted at Bemidji Teacher's College in Bemidji, Minnesota, where he took pre-engineering courses. But before he'd been there a year, he failed his courses and flunked out.

At age nineteen, Gary Paulsen enlisted in the army—and spent, he wrote later, "three years, eight months, twenty-one days, and nine hours regretting it."[1] He was sent to Colorado for basic training. Taking orders didn't come naturally to Paulsen; "I was a rebel,"[2] he later said. But his drill instructor,

Sergeant Gross, immediately challenged his defiant attitude. Gross didn't just punish Paulsen for stepping out of line; he also insisted that the young soldier was wasting his potential and encouraged him to become certified as a field engineer.

When Paulsen was finally discharged from the army in 1962, he was not in good emotional shape. "I did not think I could salvage the time I had just wasted, or that I could save my ruined life," he wrote in a memoir, *Caught by the Sea*.[3] As he had done when he was younger, Paulsen turned to the wilderness. But this time it wasn't the woods of Minnesota. It was the sea. He drove from El Paso, Texas, straight to the California coast and spent six days and nights alone by the water. "I walked until I could see the water coming in, rolling in from the vastness," he wrote, "and I sat down and let the sea heal me."[4]

Despite Paulsen's distaste for the army, it was the training he'd received there that kept him employed for the next three years. With his engineering experience, Paulsen was able to get jobs at aerospace companies. While he was working for the Goldstone Deep Space Tracking Center in California, he read a magazine article on the flight-testing of a new airplane. The article changed his life. Reading had been important to Paulsen since he was a teenager, but now, for the first time, he realized that a person—someone like the author of the article he was reading—could actually make a living as a writer. He quit his job that night, dropped his company car off at a gas station, and left town for Hollywood, determined to learn to write.

Paulsen knew nothing about writing, and he thought that the best way to learn would be to learn how to edit. After typing up a fairly creative résumé, he got a job at a men's magazine. It turned out that Paulsen had been right—editing was an excellent way to learn to write. "Editing taught me to get to the point with words," he told Leonard Marcus in an interview for the book *Author Talk*. "And it taught me that writing isn't about ego but about getting the words right."[5] During the day, Paulsen would spend time at the magazine, and at night, he would go home to work on his own writing. The next day, he would bring in whatever he had been working on and his colleagues at the magazine would critique his work. Then Paulsen would go home to write some more.

Writing was not the only thing Paulsen learned to do in Hollywood. He also had his first encounter with something that would become a lifelong obsession: boats. Just as he had gotten a magazine job without having any idea of how to write or edit, Paulsen bought a boat, got on board, began to figure out how to sail—and promptly fell overboard.

Paulsen would later call his first sailing trip "a series of calamities punctuated by terror."[6] In the harbor at Ventura, California, he decided to take the boat out to open water. But the instant he got the mainsail up, the boat took off so quickly with the wind that Paulsen was dumped over the side and watched his new boat sail off without him. Fortunately, it didn't go far before hitting the rocky shoreline, narrowly missing another boat. Paulsen swam over, climbed aboard, and got the boat headed back toward the mouth of the harbor. On the way, he hit the boat that his sailboat—sailing without him—had missed earlier. He ran into two other boats by the end of that day and still didn't make it out of the harbor.

Paulsen slept on the boat that night and woke up as the tide turned. The moonlit night was so beautiful he couldn't stand to waste it sleeping. He took his boat out into the open sea and sailed until dawn, when the wind died, leaving him stranded 12 miles (19.3 kilometers) offshore. Paulsen knew so little about the sea that he didn't notice the growing swells or the wind picking up. He didn't notice that the seabirds had all gone to the sheltered side of nearby islands to ride out the storm they knew was coming. In fact, he didn't realize that he was in any danger until a blast of wind knocked the boat sideways.

The boat stayed on its side, held down by the weight of the sails, while waves threatened to sweep Paulsen out of the cockpit. Tying a rope around his chest, he crawled out onto the deck, hanging on to whatever he could, and managed to drag down both sails, which brought the boat more or less right-side-up in the water. Somehow, the boat seemed able to keep itself upright. Exhausted, Paulsen stumbled below and fell asleep—only to be woken by a huge wave that slammed down on the boat and filled the cabin with water. He had forgotten to put the boards in place that would close off the interior of the vessel and keep it dry. Paulsen pumped the water out, put up the boards, and fell asleep again. He woke up hours later to a bright, sunny morning.

Although he didn't know it, Paulsen had been blown about 100 (161 km) miles down the coast of California, and he was now caught in a current that would eventually take him another 150 miles (241 km) south. Nevertheless, he eventually managed to get back home, learning to sail his new boat along the way.

However, despite his pleasure in sailing, Paulsen was finding it hard to concentrate on his writing in Hollywood. After a year, he moved to a small cabin in Minnesota, for which he paid twenty-five dollars a week in rent. Finally, in 1967, he sold his first book, *Some Birds Don't Fly*, a work of nonfiction for adults. It was followed shortly afterward by his first book for younger readers, *Mr. Tucket*, published by a company called Funk & Wagnalls.

Mr. Tucket is an adventure novel about a fourteen-year-old boy kidnapped from his wagon train by a Cheyenne raiding party and rescued by a mountain man, Mr. Grimes. The book didn't earn a lot of critical acclaim. In a study of Paulsen's life and work called *Presenting Gary Paulsen*, writer Gary Salvner admitted that *Mr. Tucket* is "a cliché-filled and predictable Western, certainly not one of Gary

Paulsen's better works."[7] But even with its flaws, *Mr. Tucket* was Gary Paulsen's first step toward a lifelong career of writing for young adults.

5 Discovering Dogs

With the publication of his first two books, Paulsen's writing career seemed ready to take off. He moved to Taos, New Mexico, and settled down to work as a writer. But a problem interfered. As both of his parents had done, Paulsen began to drink too much. For the next six years, he struggled with a serious alcohol problem. And he wasn't able to sell another book. Instead, he worked construction and demolition jobs to make ends meet.

One good thing did come of his years in Taos: Paulsen met Ruth Wright. She was an artist and former art teacher, and she and Paulsen were married on May 5, 1971. Their son, Jim, was born that same year. Paulsen had been married and divorced twice before, including once while he was in the army—a marriage that ended when Paulsen made his sudden decision to move to California and become a writer. His second brief marriage took place while he lived in Hollywood. Paulsen had two children with his first wife, but he lost touch with them "through [his] own stupidity,"[1] as he later admitted; both children were adopted by their mother's second husband. Paulsen and Ruth are still married.

Finally, in 1973, with the help of Alcoholics Anonymous, Paulsen was able to quit drinking for good. But it took him two years to sell another book. *The Building a New, Buying an Old, Remodeling a Used, Comprehensive Home and Shelter How-to-Do-It Book* was published in 1976. A year later, his young adult novel *Winterkill* was also published. It seemed as if Paulsen's life might be back on track at last. But in 1979, he was sued for libel by a man who thought he recognized himself as one of the characters in *Winterkill*. The lawsuit was eventually dismissed, but the experience left Paulsen so bitter and angry that he almost gave up writing entirely.

Financially, life was a struggle, especially now that Paulsen had a family to support. Finally, in 1979, things hit rock bottom. All Paulsen had in the world was $900 in cash and a car that was about to be repossessed. In an effort to live as cheaply as possible, Paulsen, Ruth, and Jim moved to a cabin outside of Bemidji, Minnesota. They had, as Paulsen said, "no plumbing, no electricity, and no real prospects."[2] Soon after, someone gave Paulsen a gift. Knowing that he had no car and no means of transportation, a friend gave him a broken-down sled and four sled dogs—Storm, Yogi, Obeah, and Columbia. Paulsen had owned many dogs since his first, Snowball. Indeed, he believes that dogs are "mandatory for decent human life."[3] But his first team of sled dogs would change his life in ways he never anticipated.

Paulsen repaired the sled, and, as he'd taught himself to sail, he taught himself to run a dog team. The dogs made it much easier for him to trap beaver. But they also helped him discover a new way of looking at the wilderness. Paulsen had spent much of his life outdoors, hunting, fishing, camping, and sailing. But working with the dogs brought him to a new understanding of the natural world.

Just as his first dog, Snowball, had taught him new ways to observe the world around him, the sled dogs helped him see the beauty of the Minnesota woods in winter. "I would see a thing of beauty when running [the dogs]," he wrote in a memoir, *Winterdance*, "or many things, the pictures like frozen jewelry, and there would not be so much beauty when not running them. So I ran them because I wanted to see the beauty again, find the wonderful places they could take me."[4]

As he spent more time with his dogs, his understanding of them deepened. He realized that they were not just working animals, but individuals. Some even had a sense of humor. Storm would tease Paulsen by hiding things from him—a glove liner, a roll of tape, a hat. Paulsen watched one day as Columbia played a joke on another dog, Olaf, by carefully placing a bone just beyond Olaf's reach. The dogs were also compassionate. One day Paulsen took a fall off the sled and broke his kneecap. He was in a bad situation—alone in the middle of a Minnesota winter, a long way from home, unable to walk. The dogs were gone; sled dogs usually do not stop when their driver falls off. They are bred to run and love to run, and they will keep going. But this time, Paulsen's dogs didn't keep going. They came back for him, let him get on the sled, and brought him back home. Paulsen was amazed that the dogs had grasped the situation, realized that he needed help, and figured out how to give it to him. He began to understand that he could learn from them.

His experiences with his sled dogs changed one fundamental thing about Paulsen: He stopped hunting and trapping. He had spent much of his life up until that point killing animals for food and money. But after getting to know his dogs, Paulsen began to realize that human beings are not separate from and superior to animals. Killing anything—even killing to eat—became repulsive to him. "I began to have a real feeling for the true sanctity of life, began to understand that life is all the cosmos gives and that to remove it, from anything, is incorrect," he wrote in *Winterdance*.[5]

Although he had stopped trapping animals, Paulsen continued to run his dogs over his old trapline. One night, Paulsen paused at the edge of a frozen lake where he always turned to go home. The dogs waited, expecting the command "Haw" for a left turn. Instead, Paulsen told them, "Gee"—the command for right. They took off down a frozen river with no plan other than to see what was around the next bend. Paulsen ran the dogs for four days. (He didn't think his wife would worry, but he was wrong; Ruth thought he had died and called friends to search for his body.) For three days, Paulsen was accompanied by a small coyote who followed the dog team. A chickadee perched on the rim of his parka hood and stayed there for half a day, eating bits of meat from his fingers. Paulsen found a deer caught in an illegal snare, a steel cable around its neck, and set it free. And he experienced "a fundamental change" in how he saw the world. "I did not elevate myself any longer, nor did I put the other aspects of nature down," he wrote. "It became, truly, we."[6]

This wild, unplanned run with his dogs was later part of the inspiration for the novel *Dogsong*. When a young Inuit boy named Russel cannot feel at home in his village, where snowmobiles whine outside his window and his father struggles with alcoholism, he takes a team of sled dogs out into the Alaskan wilderness on a run that, the village wise man tells him, will help him find his "song"—the truth about himself. Paulsen writes about Russel's run with the dogs in words that echo his own experience:

Out.

Into the sweeps, into the great places where the land runs to the sky and into the sky until there is no land and there is no sky.

Out.

Into the distance where all lines end and all lines begin. Into the white line of the ice-blink where the mother of wind lives to send down the white death of the northern storms.

Out.

Into the mother of wind and the father of blue ice.

Russel went out where there is nothing, into the wide center of everything there is.

Into the north.[7]

When Paulsen finally arrived home from the run, his wife saw him and came outside to meet him with a cup of hot soup in her hands. She asked him a question. Was he going to run the Iditarod?

Paulsen said yes.

6 The Race

The Iditarod Trail Sled Dog Race starts in Anchorage, on the southern coast of Alaska, and ends in Nome, on the western coast, covering a large portion of the state and crossing the Alaska Range along the way. It is 1,180 miles (1,899 km) long, and it is one of the most difficult and daunting races in the world.

Although Paulsen had been working with dogs for some time, racing a dog team is different—in the same ways that riding a workhorse around a farm is different from running a thoroughbred in the Kentucky Derby. As usual, Paulsen plunged right in. He knew that he would need more dogs; you must have between seven and twenty dogs to run the Iditarod. He got them anywhere he could find

51

them. Some he bought with money that he'd earned from writing and trapping, others were gifts from friends. Then he set about making the dogs and himself into a racing team.

On one of his first attempts, he harnessed the dogs to an old bicycle because there was no snow on which to run the sled. The dogs were much more powerful than he expected, but they managed to pull the bike, with Paulsen on it, out of the driveway and onto the road without disaster. Everything seemed to be going well— until the dogs spotted a rabbit and dragged Paulsen, bicycle and all, into the woods in pursuit of it.

Later, Paulsen built a rig, a tricycle-like contraption that used the wheels from an old wheelbarrow. But he didn't know that you shouldn't harness more than four or five dogs to such a light load. He spent a good portion of the time being dragged out of the yard on his face, hanging onto the rig for dear life. Once, a packet of matches in his pocket ignited from the friction. Finally, Paulsen figured out that the dogs were too powerful for the light loads he had them pulling. He solved the problem by going to the dump and finding a car without an engine. It turned out that the dogs could pull it easily.

Paulsen trained the dogs at night, when it was cooler. This had one major drawback: Skunks are nocturnal, and there are plenty of skunks in the Minnesota woods. One night, when Paulsen came home after encountering several skunks, Ruth asked him to sleep in the kennel. Paulsen realized that this was actually an opportunity: If he lived with the dogs, he would begin to learn how they thought. "I read in the kennel, sewed in the kennel, slept, and even set up a bathroom and did that in the kennel," he wrote in *Winterdance*.[1]

Training the dogs was only one of Paulsen's challenges. The Iditarod costs money. Paulsen not only had to pay the entry fees, but he also had to buy dogs and equipment and then transport the dogs, equipment, and himself to Alaska and back. Although his finances were in better shape than they had been a few years before in 1979, Paulsen could never have afforded this on his own. But his neighbors in the nearby town of Bemidji, Minnesota, pitched in. Wanting to help Paulsen achieve his dream, the townspeople donated gear, dogs, dog food, and cash. Picnics, potluck dinners, and dances were held to raise money, and businesses set up collection jars for donations. People would stop

Paulsen on the street and hand him money, saying simply, "For the race."

Paulsen was so busy training that he had no time for writing. That's what he told his editor, Richard Jackson of Bradbury Press, when Jackson called to ask what Paulsen was working on. When Paulsen confessed his financial difficulties, Jackson sent him a check, on the condition that Paulsen would send him whatever he wrote next.

At last, Paulsen and the dogs were ready for Alaska. A friend who had donated a 1968 Chevy pickup truck decided to join Paulsen for the drive north. It took eight days, as Paulsen and his friend drove without stopping, pulling a trailer with twenty sled dogs who had to be let out every four hours. At the banquet before the race began, Paulsen was unofficially voted "the least likely to get out of Anchorage."[2] This turned out to be nearly accurate. At the last minute, Paulsen decided to switch lead dogs. The lead dog is the first in the team and directs the other dogs. Paulsen normally ran with a female dog named Cookie as his lead. She was astonishingly smart; Paulsen considered her "a good friend, a kind of dogsister or dogmother."[3] But Cookie had never experienced anything like the chaos of the start of the Iditarod, and Paulsen worried that she might panic. Instead, he put a dog named Wilson in front. Two blocks into the race, Wilson missed the first turn and took Paulsen and the rest of the dog team on an impromptu tour of downtown Anchorage. Shortly after this, just outside of Anchorage, Paulsen took a wrong turn. This not only took him 60 miles (96.5 km) out of his way, but led the twenty-seven teams behind him down the wrong path as well.

Eventually, Paulsen got back on the right track, and by the time he'd reached the first of the eighteen checkpoints that a racer, or musher, must pass, the experience of running the Iditarod was already starting to affect him. "I thought my whole life had changed," he wrote in *Winterdance*, "that my basic understanding of values had changed, that I wasn't sure if I would ever recover, that I had seen god and he was a dog-man and that nothing, ever, would be the same for me again, and it was only the first true checkpoint of the race."[4]

Before the race was over, Paulsen would experience hallucinations from sleep deprivation. He would see things that weren't there, including a naked woman, the ocean off the coast of California with surfers on the waves, and a man in a trench coat who rode on his sled and was talking about federal education grants. He would think seriously about quitting. He would be attacked by a moose and would watch that moose kill the lead dog of the sled behind him. He would run through a herd of caribou and see buffalo playing games on the ice of a frozen lake. He would watch a man kill one of his own dogs, deliberately kicking it to death. (The man was later disqualified from the race when Paulsen told what he had seen.) He would eat nineteen bowls of moose chili at a checkpoint. And he would run the dogs through wind so strong that it blew them, the sled, and Paulsen off the trail, and drove sharp pieces of snow underneath his eyelids. He would run the dogs through weather so cold that his cheeks, fingers, and toes were frostbitten, and his matches would not strike.

He would lose track of time, running for hours across the vast, frozen beauty of the Alaskan wilderness, until modern life seemed unreal. "I have changed," he wrote, "moved back in time, have entered an altered state, a primitive state . . . We could run forever into this wind, across the short grass, run for all the time there has been and all the time there will be."[5] When Paulsen at last reached the end of the race, he stopped, looking at the lights of Nome, Alaska, and didn't want it to be over. Exhausted, filthy, starving, and half-frozen, all he wanted to do was turn the dogs around and run some more. Run further. Run long.

7 Running Long

The book Paulsen had promised to Richard Jackson of Bradbury Press became *Dancing Carl,* a story about a veteran of World War II, emotionally damaged by his wartime experiences, who expresses his feelings by "dancing" at the local ice rink. Shortly after this, Paulsen wrote *Popcorn Days and Buttermilk Nights,* and in 1984 came *Tracker,* based on his boyhood experience of following a deer until he was close enough to touch it.

Paulsen's standing as a writer of young adult literature was growing. Although *School Library Journal* thought that *Dancing Carl* was "lacking in action,"[1] *Horn Book Magazine* disagreed. "Filled with poetry and with life," a reviewer wrote, "the book is not only an insightful, beautifully written story for children, but for readers of any age."[2] *Horn Book Magazine* also praised *Tracker*, saying, "The simple narrative expands effortlessly to address questions of spiritual growth without losing the immediacy of plot and characters."[3] But it was Paulsen's next book, *Dogsong*, that would add enormously to his reputation.

Written while he was training for his second Iditarod, *Dogsong* draws on Paulsen's experiences running dogs in Minnesota and Alaska. It is a poetic tribute to the connection between a boy and his dog team, between the past and the present, and between humanity and nature. It was widely praised for its combination of gritty adventure and beautiful writing. *School Library Journal* called it "unusual and moving" and "a remarkable book."[4] The *Bulletin of the Center for Children's Books*, another review magazine, thought it was "slow-moving, but effective in its starkness and intensity."[5] And *Horn Book* said that Paulsen "succeeds in giving the brutal North a poetry of its own."[6] *Dogsong* would become a Newbery Honor book, and its success finally brought Paulsen some financial security.

In 1985, Paulsen made a second attempt at the Iditarod, but in the end, the weather was so bad he couldn't see his team in front of him, and snow and ice blew into his eyes even though they were closed. Ultimately, the wind blew his dogs back on top of him in "a furry pile."[7] Close to the end of the race he got word to Nome that he needed to be picked up, and a small plane came to get him.

Two years later, in 1987, *Hatchet* was published. And something extraordinary happened. *Hatchet* is, in essence, a fairly simple story. Thirteen-year-old Brian Robeson is stranded by a plane crash in the Canadian wilderness and must survive on his own for fifty-four days until he is rescued. By paying attention to his surroundings and remembering facts and lessons from his earlier life, Brian masters the skills he needs to survive:

> He would not forget his first hit. Not ever. A round-shaped fish, with golden sides, sides as gold as the sun, stopped in front of the arrow and he aimed just beneath it, at the bottom edge of the fish, and released the arrow and there was a bright flurry, a splash of gold in the water. He grabbed the arrow and raised it up and the fish was on the end, wiggling against the blue sky.

He held the fish against the sky until it stopped wiggling, held it and looked to the sky and felt his throat tighten, swell, and fill with pride at what he had done.

He had done food.[8]

Hatchet was more than a critical and popular success. It was a phenomenon. There have been many adventure and survival novels about protagonists who must struggle to live in the wilderness. But *Hatchet*, with its precise details based on Paulsen's own experiences, and its profound sense of respect for the natural world, touched a nerve with an astonishing number of readers. Although some reviewers criticized a subplot involving the divorce of Brian's parents, finding it contrived or undeveloped, they were otherwise universal in their praise. The *Bulletin of the Center for Children's Books* called *Hatchet* "deftly conceived and developed."[9] "Paulsen emphasizes character growth through a careful balancing of specific details of survival with the protagonist's thoughts and emotions," wrote a reviewer for *School Library Journal*.[10]

Hatchet won Paulsen a second Newbery Honor. Suddenly, he was in demand as a speaker at schools and writers' conferences. He received countless letters from young readers (and some older ones as well) who longed to know what happened to Brian after he was rescued. In the end, these letters resulted in three more novels about Brian and a memoir, *Guts*, describing events in Paulsen's own life that Brian's adventures are based on.

Paulsen continued to write, publishing his third Newbery Honor book, *The Winter Room*, in 1989. He also continued to run dogs, planning for his third Iditarod. But his plans didn't work out. In 1990, he experienced chest pains and was told by a doctor that he had heart disease. It was not immediately fatal, and with a careful diet Paulsen could expect to live many more years. But his body couldn't take the stress of running dogs anymore. From the hospital where he had received the diagnosis, Paulsen called a friend who also ran dogs and told him to take everything—all the dogs, all the gear. By the time he got home from the hospital, the only thing left from what had been the focus of his life for nine years was his beloved lead dog, Cookie.

Cookie had arthritis and had stopped racing not long before Paulsen was diagnosed with heart disease. She moved from the kennel into the house, where she promptly killed and ate one of Ruth Paulsen's cats. After coming home from the hospital, Paulsen spent most of his time at home. Cookie hardly left his side until her death.

At first, Paulsen thought that his diagnosis of heart disease meant the end of everything he loved. But he wasn't capable of giving up. Without the dogs, he found that Minnesota winters were "not nearly as interesting."[11] He decided to move south. First, he and Ruth tried Wyoming, living in a small cabin at the foot of the Bighorn Mountains. There he discovered that, although he couldn't race sled dogs anymore, he wasn't cut off from the wilderness after all. He bought two horses, Merry and Blackie, and began to explore the mountains. "Since diagnosed with heart disease I have seen cliff dwellings and deserts and mountains . . . have dodged bear and been bit by snakes . . . and seen sunsets and dawns that no man, ever, has seen before or will see again in the same way or place," he wrote.[12]

Wyoming, as it turned out, wasn't south enough. For a couple of years, Gary and Ruth moved back and forth between New Mexico and Minnesota. Eventually, in 1992, they settled in La Luz, New Mexico. There, Paulsen did something he'd wanted to do all his life: He bought a Harley-Davidson motorcycle. Then he took his new bike on a little ride—a twelve-day, 9,000-mile (1,484 km) trip from New Mexico to Alaska and back. Paulsen found that "there is something very liberating about heart disease." He discovered that many of the things people think are important—"car payments, careers, lawyers, awards, families"—don't really matter. What matters is simply one thing: that you live life "the best way you know how."[13]

In New Mexico, Paulsen rekindled his love for the sea. After his motorcycle trip to Alaska, Paulsen bought an old sailboat, *Felicity*, and sailed up and down the West Coast of North America. Off the Alaskan coast, he sat at anchor while humpback whales fed nearby, "so close they could be touched, turning gently so that their flukes would not hit the boat, missing by inches, with killer whales mugging and fighting and playing around the boat in the clear, cold water."[14]

Later, Paulsen bought a new boat, a catamaran, called the *Ariel*. "Lord, she jumped out, seemed to leap forward with me," Paulsen remembered about the first time he took the *Ariel* to sea, "jumping from wave to wave, flat and fast and leaving little rooster tails in back of her two hulls like a speed boat."[15] Paulsen made several trips on the *Ariel* in the late 1990s, sailing to Hawaii, Samoa, Fiji, and back to Mexico. He hopes to sail around Cape Horn, the southern tip of South America.

He also continued to write. Few writers have been so prolific or have written in such a wide variety of styles. He has written both fiction and nonfiction, and his books include memoirs, survival stories, historical fiction, science fiction, picture books, and the Gary Paulsen World of Adventure and Culpepper Adventure series. Altogether he has published over 100 books and sees no end in sight.

"I had to run long," Paulsen wrote about his motorcycle trip from New Mexico to Alaska.

> I had learned that from the dogs. Whether it's love or work or laughter or pain or hate you cannot know it unless you run long, stay with it past the first flush, get over the mountain range and learn what it's truly like.[16]

Whether he's writing books, running dogs, sailing, or riding a motorcycle, Gary Paulsen doesn't stop easily. He runs long.

8 A Pilgrimage to Seek

In 1997, Gary Paulsen won the Margaret A. Edwards Award. Unlike many awards, which are given to a single book, the Edwards Award honors a writer's lifetime contribution to the field of young adult literature. Regarding Paulsen, the chair of the Edward Committee said:

> From quiet introspective memoirs to edge-of-the-seat adventures, Paulsen grabs and holds the attention of his readers. The theme of survival is woven throughout, whether it is living through a plane crash or living in an abusive, alcoholic household . . . With his intense love of the outdoors and crazy courage born of adversity, Paulsen has reached young adults everywhere. His writing conveys a profound respect for their intelligence and ability to overcome life's worst realities.[1]

Paulsen writes about survival. In book after book, his main characters find themselves facing dangerous situations, and readers keep turning the pages to discover if they will make it. Will Brian be rescued from the wilderness? Will Francis of *Mr. Tucket* make it to Oregon and find his family again? Paulsen's clean, direct style is well-suited to his action-filled plots, and easily pulls a reader in. "Stark and bareboned," a reviewer for the *Bulletin of the Center for Children's Books* described his prose, "without stylistic pretensions of any kind."[2]

The challenges in Paulsen's books are never simply physical. *Children's Literature Review* has said that Paulsen "balances the characteristic action of his works by probing the thoughts and emotions of his characters as they move on inner journeys toward self-discovery."[3] The emotional and mental aspects of survival give Paulsen's books depth. His characters endure plane crashes, storms at sea, poverty, war, and slavery; they also face isolation, the neglect or abuse of parents, and the deaths of loved ones. Forced to encounter difficulties that are both physical and psychological, they make it— they survive.

But Paulsen is not blindly optimistic; indeed, he is unflinchingly honest about life's difficult realities. The wilderness so many of his characters encounter may be a beautiful place, but life there is never easy. Paulsen doesn't flinch from telling his readers about his difficult childhood or his parents' alcoholism or his heart disease. He is uncompromising in showing the devastation of war or the brutality of slavery. "These matter-of-fact descriptions of human misery and senseless torture are probably unlike anything this age group has read or heard about,"[4] a reviewer for *School Library Journal* wrote of *Nightjohn*. With his sometimes brutal honesty, Paulsen is a writer that readers can trust.

Paulsen's honesty is matched by a sharp eye for detail that makes his scenes vividly realistic. In *Hatchet*, for example, Brian spends six pages trying to light a fire without a match, each painstaking step described with such precision that readers feel as if they are there, watching Brian's struggle. Paulsen's writing is so convincing, in fact, that after *Hatchet* was published, the National Geographic Society called him to ask if they could interview Brian. When Paulsen told them that the story was fiction, that he had made Brian up, at first they didn't believe him. It seemed impossible that there wasn't a "real Brian."

Paulsen is careful to foster his appetite and memory for the kind of detail that convinces readers. He takes trips alone so that he can pay careful attention to his surroundings; he describes his attention as "wolflike."[5] In his historical novels, careful research takes the place of personal experience. It took Paulsen five years to do the research for the ninety-two-page novel *Nightjohn*.

Paulsen's love and respect for the natural world also brings readers to his work. "The lure of the wilderness is always a potent draw," a reviewer for *Horn Book Magazine* wrote, "and Paulsen evokes its mysteries as well as anyone since Jack London."[6] His characters come to understand the wilderness, and the lesson reverberates with force for his readers because Paulsen himself feels it so deeply. "While many adventure writers establish conflicts in their books that are resolved by a protagonist learning to subdue or conquer the natural world," Gary Salvner wrote in *Presenting Gary Paulsen*, "Paulsen's protagonists survive because they learn to respect it."[7]

Toward the end of *Hatchet,* Brian recovers a rifle from the airplane's survival pack. But by this time he feels so close to the wilderness that he is uncomfortable with the weapon. It will make his life much easier, and yet it will also separate him from his surroundings.

> It somehow removed him from everything around him. Without the rifle he had to fit in, to be part of it all, to understand it and use it—the woods, all of it. With the rifle, suddenly, he didn't have to know; did not have to be afraid or understand . . . The rifle changed him, the minute he picked it up, and he wasn't sure he liked the change very much.[8]

To respect the natural world means being open to the lessons it can teach. Paulsen has called the act of learning "the maximum expression of being human,"[9] and he himself has never stopped; he learned to hunt, sail, race a team of sled dogs, and write professionally. He learned from books, mentors, his sled dogs, and the world around him. His characters survive by gaining knowledge—knowledge about the wilderness and knowledge about themselves. Some of this knowledge they acquire by experience; some they find by listening to and learning from others. In *Nightjohn*, a twelve-year-old slave girl, Sarny, risks her life to learn to read and write in order to pass her knowledge on to others. Sarny's caretaker asks her teacher, Nightjohn, why Sarny and others should try to learn. "They have to be able to write," Nightjohn answers. "They have to read and write. We all have to read and write so we can write about this— what they doing to us. It has to be written."[10]

In 1997, when he won the Edwards Award, Paulsen knew he had many more books left to write. At the time, he said he was probably "a hundred books behind."[11] If Paulsen isn't writing a new book, he's planning one, and if he isn't traveling he's planning a trip. This restless energy fills his writing. Paulsen's books sweep readers in from the first sentence and hurry them along with plots full of action. Reading his work, you get the feeling that this is not a man with time to waste. He has somewhere to go and is willing to take his readers with him— whether it's on a dogsled to Nome or a sea voyage to Cape Horn. And the journey itself matters more than the destination, because the journey is where you meet new experiences. The journey is how you learn.

"To seek. Not to find, not to end, but to always seek a beginning," Paulsen wrote about his motorcycle trip to Alaska. "That was what the trip had become for me—as the Iditarods had been, and all my life had been, though I had not seen it, not understood it—a pilgrimage only to seek."[12]

Interview with Gary Paulsen

SARAH L. THOMSON: You did badly in school, dropped out of college—and now you're a writer. How did that happen? How did it occur to you that writing was something you could learn to do, and something that you wanted to do?

GARY PAULSEN: I hated school, hated it, was a terrible student, but, after I was about fourteen, I loved reading. I've talked many times about how a librarian handed me a book when I was a kid. She saved me, she really did, by giving me that book. She turned me into a reader, made me love reading and books and stories.

I didn't know I would write books, though, until many years later, after I'd barely passed high school and dropped out of college and joined the army and gotten married and had two kids and was working for an aerospace company, tracking satellites. Late one night, it came to me, as suddenly as that, I have to write. I just knew that I had to be a writer, that there was nothing else on this earth for me to do with my life. I quit my job that night, went home and told my wife that I was giving up my job to be a writer and, then, after she left me (we had a difference of opinion about the wisdom of my decision, to put it mildly), I went to California to apprentice myself to people who could teach me how to write. I worked on a men's magazine, oddly enough, where a few writers helped me to learn how to make words dance.

SARAH L. THOMSON: Are there writers you remember reading as a young adult whose work was formative for you when you began to write your own books?

GARY PAULSEN: I don't remember any specific authors I read, but I loved science fiction when I was young. Later I tried my hand at that genre with *The Transall Saga*. I loved Westerns, too, when I first started to read. After a while, I'd read anything and I'm still like that. I have to read every morning when I wake up and every night before I go to sleep and, since I'm living on a boat and my access to stores and libraries is limited, I pretty much pick up any book I find in marinas and other people's boats and read anything I can.

SARAH L. THOMSON: Does your writing process change depending on whether you're writing fiction or nonfiction? Do you like writing one better than the other?

GARY PAULSEN: I don't really think of writing fiction or nonfiction—I write to tell stories, to dance with words, and I find that process fascinating no matter the subject or the inspiration. I write the same way all the time—anywhere and everywhere I can, longhand in notebooks or at my computer in my office or on a laptop wherever I am. I wrote *Dogsong* by the light of a headlamp in dog kennels at night, and I wrote *Nightjohn* in my basement at an old table, and I wrote *Guts* on a laptop in hotels as I was on tour to promote another book, and I wrote *Caught by the Sea* in the galley of my sailboat waiting out storms.

SARAH L. THOMSON: Can you tell us something about the reader response to *Hatchet*? Do you have any idea why this book in particular has struck a chord with so many readers?

GARY PAULSEN: I don't know why so many young readers like *Hatchet*. I'm always surprised by how many letters I get about Brian and his adventures. The letters, in fact, are the reasons I wrote the sequels—*The River*, *Brian's Winter*, and *Brian's Return* were all written in response to the letters I've received, trying to answer the many questions kids have asked me about Brian.

SARAH L. THOMSON: How many drafts do you do of a novel? How do you know when you're done?

GARY PAULSEN: I work on a book so many times in my head before I ever sit down to write it that I usually have the entire book plotted out in detail. I can tell you what page sixty-seven will look like, down to the paragraph spacing. So when I actually sit down to type or write the book, I just need the one draft to get down on paper what I've been working on in my head. Keep in mind, though, that I've been writing books for thirty years now and have written hundreds of books and I spend months—years, sometimes—chewing away at different story ideas before I ever start to write them. So the work is there, just not in draft form.

SARAH L. THOMSON: What is your relationship with your editor like? Is it difficult to have your work edited?

GARY PAULSEN: I have the greatest editors. Dick Jackson, David Gale, and now Wendy Lamb are three of the best in the business. They make it easy to work with them and, no, I have no problem being edited. They've become dear friends to me and great supporters, my first supporters, of my books.

SARAH L. THOMSON: Which of your books was the easiest to write?

GARY PAULSEN: I think *Harris and Me* was the easiest book to write because I just sat down and remembered all the trouble Harlan (that was Harris's real name) and I got into when I was a boy. The stories just kept coming to me and I kept writing them down as fast as I could. It was good to remember that happy time in my childhood and that made the work easy.

SARAH L. THOMSON: You've written picture books and books for adults, but the bulk of your writing has been for young adults. Is there a reason you like writing for this particular audience?

GARY PAULSEN: I write for young people because they are so open to the idea of story. They're not like adults worrying about mortgages and divorces and their cars. They open themselves up to books in a way that is wonderful. I always say that every good thing happened to me because of kids and dogs and librarians.

SARAH L. THOMSON: What's the most beautiful place you have ever been?

GARY PAULSEN: The most beautiful place I have ever seen is the South Pacific, from the back of a sailboat.

SARAH L. THOMSON: When are you going to sail around Cape Horn?

GARY PAULSEN: As soon as the boat is ready and the wind and weather are favorable.

Timeline

1939 Gary Paulsen is born on May 17.

1944 Paulsen and his mother move to Chicago, Illinois.

1945 Paulsen and his mother join his father in the Philippines.

1949 The Paulsen family returns to the United States.

1957 Paulsen graduates from high school.

1959 Paulsen enlists in the army.

1962 Paulsen is discharged from the army. He goes to work for aerospace firms in California.

1965 Paulsen moves to Hollywood, California, and finds work as an editor at a men's magazine.

1966 Paulsen moves back to northern Minnesota. His first book, *Some Birds Don't Fly*, is published.

1967 Paulsen moves to Taos, New Mexico.

1968 Paulsen's first young adult novel, *Mr. Tucket*, is published.

1971 Paulsen marries Ruth Wright.

1976 *Winterkill* is published.

1979 Paulsen and his family move back to Minnesota.

1980 Paulsen begins to run dogs.

1983 Paulsen races in the Iditarod.

1985 Paulsen races in his second Iditarod.

1985 *Dogsong* is published.

1987 *Hatchet* is published.

1989 *The Winter Room* is published.

1990 Paulsen is diagnosed with heart trouble. He gives up running dogs.

1992 Paulsen moves to La Luz, New Mexico.

1993 Paulsen drives a motorcycle to Alaska.

1997 Paulsen wins the Margaret A. Edwards Award.

Selected Reviews from *School Library Journal*

Hatchet
December 1987

Gr 8–12—Brian Robeson, thirteen, is the only passenger on a small plane flying him to visit his father in the Canadian wilderness when the pilot has a heart attack and dies. The plane drifts off course and finally crashes into a small lake. Miraculously Brian is able to swim free of the plane, arriving on a sandy tree-lined shore with only his clothing, a tattered windbreaker, and the hatchet his mother had given him as a present. The novel chronicles in gritty detail Brian's mistakes, setbacks, and small triumphs as, with the help of the hatchet, he manages to survive the fifty-four days alone in the wilderness. Paulsen effectively shows readers how Brian learns patience to watch, listen, and think before he acts as he attempts to build a fire, to fish and hunt, and to make his home under a rock overhang safe and comfortable. An epilogue discussing the lasting effects of Brian's stay in the wilderness and his dim chance of survival had winter come upon him before rescue adds credibility to the story. Paulsen tells a fine adventure story, but the sub-plot concerning Brian's preoccupation with his parents' divorce seems a bit forced and detracts from the book. As he did in *Dogsong* (Bradbury, 1985), Paulsen emphasizes character growth through a careful balancing of specific details of survival with the protagonist's thoughts and emotions. —Barbara Chatton, College of Education, University of Wyoming, Laramie, Wyoming

Winterkill
November 1976

Gr 6 Up—This is a downbeat tale of a semi-delinquent boy who is befriended by a cop.

Duda, the cop, rescues the boy (whose name is never revealed) from several potentially dangerous situations, and the boy, in turn, exerts a calming influence on Duda's savage, violent streak. The shocking conclusion in which Duda is shot to death by a disturbed youth is wholly in keeping with the characters Paulsen has so painstakingly created. Narrated convincingly by its young protagonist, this is reminiscent of Hinton's *The Outsiders* (Viking, 1967) in its shattering portrayal of life on the wrong side of town. —Diane Haas, Howe Library, Hanover, New Hampshire

Brian's Return
February, 1999

Gr 6 Up—Readers who have been dissatisfied with the various endings to the story of Brian of *Hatchet* (Bradbury, 1987) fame now have another alternative ending, perhaps the one for which they've been waiting. In *Brian's Return*, Paulsen describes the boy's escalating inability to participate in modern American teenage life, climaxing in a physical confrontation outside a pizza parlor during which Brian behaves as if he's been confronted by a threatening wild animal. Sent for counseling after this incident, he realizes that he needs to return to the wild and lead an existence attuned to nature rather than MTV. This seems to be a logical conclusion for him, and readers have long since ceased to worry about this young man's ability to cope with any hazard nature may throw his way, so they can leave him in the North Woods with absolute contentment. It is a relief that Paulsen's considerable talents are now freed to address other subjects. —Miriam Lang Budin, Mt. Kisco Public Library, New York

The Winter Room
October, 1989

Gr 6–9—Of the four rooms downstairs in the northern Minnesota farmhouse, the one that might be called a living room is where Wayne and Eldon, their parents and great-uncle, and old Norwegian Nels spend their winters. There the family sits near the corner wood stove and listens, uninterrupting, as Uncle David tells stories—of the old country, of old times, of a semi-mythical lumberjack. Eldon, the younger son, begins his own story, in spring, when everything is soft. While he describes for readers the farm activities of each season and narrates memorable pranks and milestones of his boyhood, it is the palpable awareness of place and character that is unforgettable. Paulsen, with a simple intensity, brings to consciousness the texture, the smells, the light and shadows of each distinct season. He has penned a mood poem in prose. Uncle David's final story precipitates within the brothers a fuller understanding of personal identity and integrity. For those special readers who find delight in *The Winter Room*, it will become a part of their own identity and understanding. Teachers who seek to illuminate the use of ordinary English words with extraordinary descriptive power will find the intro- ductory chapter, in particular, to be a godsend. —Katharine Bruner, Brown Middle School, Harrison, Tennessee

The Monument
October 1991

Gr 6–9—Figuring she'll never get adopted because of her caramel-colored skin and crippled leg, Rocky finds herself chosen by Emma and Fred, a kind, indulgent, alcoholic couple from Bolton, Kansas. It's in Bolton that she finds her devoted dog, Python, who leads her to Mick, the rumpled artist hired to design a monument to the town's war dead and the person who changes Rocky's view of life, art, and the world. Through the drawings he makes in order to get a feel for the town's people and history, the citizens of Bolton see themselves and their surroundings in a new light, although they're not sure they like it. As Mick does with his sketches, Paulsen tells the story in quick, deft strokes. The gossip at the grain elevator on a summer day, Rocky's insecurities and toughness, and the varied characters are vividly yet succinctly conveyed. In just three days, Mick breezes into town, turns Rocky on to the power of art, and convinces the people of Bolton that a grove of trees will be an appropriate monument as well as an artistic statement. Avoiding a lot of artistic jargon, Paulsen carries readers along with his (and Mick's) strong images and enthusiasm. A powerful, affecting story with its comments on art and homage. —Susan Knorr, Milwaukee Public Library, Milwaukee, Wisconsin

Clabbered Dirt, Sweet Grass
September 1992

This is a quintessential farm story filled with images of rich soil, warm sun, strong crops, sleek animals, and the ongoing cycle of labor from plowing to harvest. The people in Paulsen's tale are incidental to the work. Up before the sun, a family of work-roughened hands are always cooking and laying table, milking and harnessing horses, repairing machinery and delicately quilting. The reader is drawn in by the words and by the paintings of Paulsen's wife, Ruth Wright Paulsen, until they too feel the sweat and the strain of muscles, the heat of summer canning, the joy of a summer picnic, the ongoing rush to have enough food and just a little money to live another year on the farm. Where Richard Rhodes's *Farm* (LJ 1/90) nails down the reality of agricultural life, Paulsen's *Clabbered Dirt, Sweet Grass* lets the reader dream of simpler, kinder times. This book is very well written and illustrated and will appeal to a general audience as well as one with a specific interest in farming or agriculture. Highly recommended. —Debra Schneider, Virginia Henderson International Nursing Library, Indianapolis, Indiana

Selected reviews from *School Library Journal* reproduced, with permission, from *School Library Journal* copyright © 1976, 1987, 1988, 1989, 1991, 1992, 1999 by Cahners Business Information, a division of Reed Elsevier, Inc.

List of
Selected Works

Alida's Song. New York: Delacorte
    Press, 1999.
*The Beet Fields: Memories of a Sixteenth
    Summer.* New York: Delacorte
    Press, 2000.
Brian's Return. New York: Delacorte
    Press, 1999.
Brian's Winter. New York: Delacorte
    Press, 1996.
Canyons. New York: Delacorte Press, 1990.
Caught by the Sea: My Life on Boats.
    New York: Delacorte Press, 2001.
The Crossing. New York: Orchard
    Books, 1987.

Dancing Carl. New York: Bradbury
    Press, 1983.
Dogsong. New York: Bradbury Press, 1985.
Eastern Sun, Winter Moon. New York: Harcourt
    Brace Jovanovich, 1993.
*Father Water, Mother Woods: Essays on Fishing
    and Hunting in the North Woods*. Illustrated
    by Ruth Wright Paulsen. New York:
    Delacorte Press, 1994.
Guts: The True Stories Behind Hatchet *and
    the Brian Books*. New York: Delacorte
    Press, 2001.
Harris and Me: A Summer Remembered. San
    Diego: Harcourt Brace & Company, 1993.
Hatchet. New York: Bradbury Press, 1987.
My Life in Dog Years. Illustrated by Ruth Wright
    Paulsen. New York: Delacorte Press, 1998.
Nightjohn. New York: Delacorte Press, 1993.
*Pilgrimage on a Steel Ride: A Memoir About Men
    and Motorcycles*. New York: Harcourt Brace
    & Company, 1997.
*Puppies, Dogs, and Blue Northers: Reflections on
    Being Raised by a Pack of Sled Dogs.*San
    Diego: Harcourt Brace & Company, 1996.
Sarny: A Life Remembered. New York: Delacorte
    Press, 1997.

Winterdance: The Fine Madness of Running the Iditarod. San Diego: A Harvest Book, Harcourt Brace & Company, 1994.

The Winter Room. New York: Orchard Books, 1989.

Woodsong. New York: Bradbury Press, 1990.

List of
Selected Awards

The Boy Who Owned the School
Parents' Choice Award (1991)

Brian's Winter
International Reading Association Young
   Adults Choice (1996)

The Cookcamp
School Library Journal Best Book of the
   Year (1991)

Dogsong
American Library Association Best Book for
   Young Adults (1985)
Newbery Honor Book (1986)
Parents' Choice Award (1985)

Dogteam
International Reading Association Children's
   Book Council, Children's Choices for 1994

Father Water, Mother Woods
Publishers Weekly Best Book of 1994

Harris and Me: A Summer Remembered
American Library Association Best Book for
   Young Adults (1993)
New York Public Library, Children's Books: 100
   Titles for Reading and Sharing (1993)

Hatchet
American Library Association Notable
  Children's Book (1987)
Booklist Editor's Choice (1988)
Newbery Honor Book (1988)

The Haymeadow
American Library Association Notable and Best
  Book (1992)

The Monument
American Library Association Best Book for
  Young Adults (1991)

My Life in Dog Years
American Library Association Quick Pick for
  Reluctant Young Adult Readers (1998)

Nightjohn
American Library Association Best Book for
  Young Adults (1993)

The River
International Reading Association Children's Book
  Council (1991)

The Winter Room
American Library Association Notable and Best
  Book (1989)
Newbery Honor Book (1990)

Woodsong
Booklist Editors' Choice CitdsAation (1991)
Spur Award, Western Writers of America (1991)

Glossary

Alaska Range   A mountain range in southeastern Alaska. It contains Mount McKinley, also known as Denali, at 20,320 feet (6,096 meters), the highest mountain in North America.

Allies   In World War II, the group of nations (including Canada, China, Great Britain, the Soviet Union, and the United States) who opposed the Axis powers (including Germany, Italy, and Japan). In 1945, the Allies were victorious.

baloot   A duck egg that is left to rot in hot sand until the unhatched body of the duckling inside is partially rotted. Baloots are considered a delicacy in the Philippines.

Cape Horn The southernmost tip of South America. To sail "around the Horn" means sailing between South America and Antarctica, through one of the stormiest regions in the world.

catamaran A raftlike boat with two hulls (the body of the boat); regular boats have a single hull. Because of their light weight and low water resistance, catamarans are known for speed.

corpsman A medic in the military, trained to perform first aid.

cosmos The universe.

ducktail A hairstyle popular for men in the 1950s; the hair was left long in back and swept up like a duck's tail.

entrails Internal organs, particularly intestines.

exchange The store on a military base.

Filipino A native of the Philippines.

flattop A short hairstyle popular for men in the 1950s.

guerrilla A member of a small band of fighters that works in secret, usually relying on hit-and-run tactics, ambushes, and sabotage.

Huk A shortened name for a member of the Hukbong Magpapalayang Bayan, or the People's Liberation Army, an armed group who tried to take over the government of the Philippines from 1949 to 1954.

Iditarod Trail Sled Dog Race   An annual dogsled race in Alaska. The Iditarod starts in Anchorage and ends 1,180 miles away, in Nome.

mainsail   The largest sail on a boat.

memoir   A writer's account of his or her own life. A memoir is usually shorter than an autobiography and often concentrates on one specific time or event rather than telling the story of the writer's entire life.

mentor   Someone who guides or teaches.

musher   A dogsled driver.

Newbery Medal   An award given every year to the most distinguished contribution to American children's literature. A number of Newbery Honor Awards (usually between two and four) are also given each year to books that the Newbery Committee considers to be of special merit.

potent   Powerful.

sanctity   The quality of being holy or sacred.

snowhook   An anchor on a dogsled that can hold the sled in place.

trapline   A series of traps to catch animals, set in an area that animals visit regularly.

For More Information

Web Sites

Due to the changing nature of Internet links, the Rosen Publishing Group, Inc., has developed an online list of Web sites related to the subject of this book. This site is updated regularly. Please use this link to access the list:

http://www.rosenlinks.com/lab/gpau/

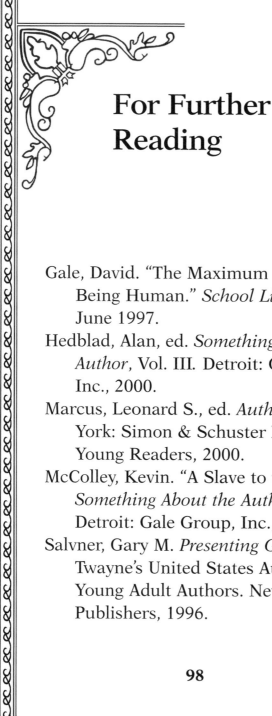

For Further Reading

Gale, David. "The Maximum Expression of Being Human." *School Library Journal*, June 1997.

Hedblad, Alan, ed. *Something About the Author*, Vol. III. Detroit: Gale Group, Inc., 2000.

Marcus, Leonard S., ed. *Author Talk.* New York: Simon & Schuster Books for Young Readers, 2000.

McColley, Kevin. "A Slave to the Dance." *Something About the Author*, Vol. 23. Detroit: Gale Group, Inc., 1997.

Salvner, Gary M. *Presenting Gary Paulsen.* Twayne's United States Author Series, Young Adult Authors. New York: Twayne Publishers, 1996.

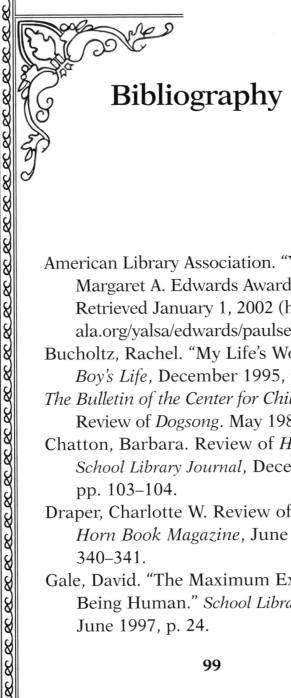

Bibliography

American Library Association. "YALSA: Margaret A. Edwards Award." 2000. Retrieved January 1, 2002 (http://www. ala.org/yalsa/edwards/paulsen.html).

Bucholtz, Rachel. "My Life's Work: Author." *Boy's Life*, December 1995, p. 28.

The Bulletin of the Center for Children's Books. Review of *Dogsong*. May 1985, p. 174.

Chatton, Barbara. Review of *Hatchet*. *School Library Journal*, December 1987, pp. 103–104.

Draper, Charlotte W. Review of *Tracker*. *Horn Book Magazine*, June 1984, pp. 340–341.

Gale, David. "The Maximum Expression of Being Human." *School Library Journal*, June 1997, p. 24.

Gardner, Jane E. Review of *Dancing Carl*. *School Library Journal*, May 1983, p. 84.

Hand, Dorcas. Review of *Dancing Carl*. *Horn Book Magazine*, August 1983, pp. 446–447.

Hearne, Betsy. Review of *Nightjohn*. *The Bulletin of the Center for Children's Books*, February 1993, pp. 187–188.

Hedblad, Alan, ed. *Something About the Author*, Vol. III, pp. 136–145. Detroit: Gale Group, Inc., 2000.

Kirkus Children's and Young Adult Edition. Review of *Hatchet*, August 1, 1987, pp. 1161–1162.

Luzer, Richard. Review of *Dogsong*. *School Library Journal*, April 1985, p. 98.

Marcus, Leonard S., ed. *Author Talk*. New York: Simon & Schuster Books for Young Readers, 2000.

Paulsen, Gary. *The Beet Fields: Memories of a Sixteenth Summer*. New York: Delacorte Press, 2000.

Paulsen, Gary. *Brian's Winter*. New York: Delacorte Press, 1996.

Paulsen, Gary. *Caught by the Sea: My Life on Boats*. New York: Delacorte Press, 2001.

Paulsen, Gary. *Dogsong*. New York: Bradbury Press, 1985.

Paulsen, Gary. *Eastern Sun, Winter Moon.* New York: Harcourt Brace Jovanovich, 1993.

Paulsen, Gary. *Father Water, Mother Woods: Essays on Fishing and Hunting in the North Woods.* Illustrated by Ruth Wright Paulsen. New York: Delacorte Press, 1994.

Paulsen, Gary. *Guts: The True Story Behind* Hatchet *and the Brian Books.* New York: Delacorte Press, 2001.

Paulsen, Gary. *Hatchet.* New York: Bradbury Press, 1987.

Paulsen, Gary. *My Life in Dog Years.* Illustrated by Ruth Wright Paulsen. New York: Delacorte Press, 1998.

Paulsen, Gary. *Nightjohn.* New York: Delacorte Press, 1993.

Paulsen, Gary. *Pilgrimage on a Steel Ride: A Memoir About Men and Motorcycles.* New York: Harcourt Brace & Company, 1997.

Paulsen, Gary. *Puppies, Dogs, and Blue Northers: Reflections on Being Raised by a Pack of Sled Dogs.* San Diego: Harcourt Brace & Company, 1996.

Paulsen, Gary. *Winterdance: The Fine Madness of Running the Iditarod.* San Diego: A Harvest Book, Harcourt Brace & Company, 1994.

Paulsen, Gary. *The Winter Room*. New York: Orchard Books, 1989.

Paulsen, Gary. *Woodsong*. New York: Bradbury Press, 1990.

Rogers, Susan L. Review of *Nightjohn*. *School Library Journal*, March 1993, p. 223.

Salvner, Gary M. *Presenting Gary Paulsen*. Twayne's United States Author Series, Young Adult Authors. New York: Twayne Publishers, 1996.

Sutherland, Zena. Review of *Hatchet*. *The Bulletin of the Center for Children's Books*, December 1987, p. 73.

Twichell, Ethel R. Review of *Dogsong*. *Horn Book Magazine*, July/August 1985, pp. 456–457.

Vasilakis, Nancy. Review of *Woodsong*. *Horn Book Magazine*, November/December 1990, p. 762.

Weidt, Maryann M. "Interview with Gary Paulsen." *Children's Literature Review*, Vol. 19, pp. 167–178. Detroit: Gale Group, Inc., 1990.

Source Notes

Introduction

1. Gary Paulsen, *Guts: The True Story Behind* Hatchet *and the Brian Books* (New York: Delacorte Press, 2001), p. 133.
2. Gary Paulsen, *Winterdance: The Fine Madness of Running the Iditarod* (San Diego, CA: A Harvest Book, Harcourt Brace & Company, 1994), p. 11.

Chapter 1

1. Gary Paulsen, *Eastern Sun, Winter Moon* (New York: Harcourt Brace Jovanovich, 1993), p. 132.

Chapter 2

1. Gary Paulsen, *My Life in Dog Years*, illustrated by Ruth Wright Paulsen (New York: Delacorte Press, 1998), p. 14.

2. Gary Paulsen, *Eastern Sun, Winter Moon* (New York: Harcourt Brace Jovanovich, 1993), p. 236.
3. Paulsen, *My Life in Dog Years*, p. 18.

Chapter 3

1. Gary Paulsen, *Father Water, Mother Woods: Essays on Fishing and Hunting in the North Woods*, illustrated by Ruth Wright Paulsen (New York: Delacorte Press, 1994), pp. xi–xii.
2. Ibid., p. 105.
3. Gary Paulsen, *The Beet Fields: Memories of a Sixteenth Summer* (New York: Delacorte Press, 2000), pp. 3–4.
4. Gary Paulsen, *The Winter Room* (New York: Orchard Books, 1989), pp. 68–69.
5. Leonard S. Marcus, ed., *Author Talk* (New York: Simon & Schuster Books for Young Readers, 2000), p. 79.
6. Alan Hedblad, ed., *Something About the Author*, Vol. 111 (Detroit: Gale Group, Inc., 2000), p. 140.
7. Gary Paulsen, *Pilgrimage on a Steel Ride: A Memoir About Men and Motorcycles* (New York: Harcourt Brace & Company, 1997), p. 64.
8. Paulsen, *Father Water, Mother Woods*, p. xii.
9. Ibid., pp. 123–124.
10. Gary Paulsen, *Guts: The True Story Behind* Hatchet *and the Brian Books* (New York: Delacorte Press, 2001), p. 70.
11. Paulsen, *Father Water, Mother Woods*, p. 133.
12. Ibid., p. 148.

Chapter 4

1. Gary Paulsen, *Winterdance: The Fine Madness of Running the Iditarod* (San Diego: A Harvest Book, Harcourt Brace & Company), p. 83.

2. Gary M. Salvner, *Presenting Gary Paulsen*, Twayne's United States Author Series, Young Adult Authors (New York: Twayne Publishers, 1996), p. 16.

3. Gary Paulsen, *Caught by the Sea: My Life on Boats* (New York: Delacorte Press), p. 5.

4. Ibid., p. 6.

5. Leonard S. Marcus, ed., *Author Talk* (New York: Simon & Schuster Books for Young Readers, 2000), p. 79.

6. Paulsen, *Caught by the Sea*, p. 28.

7. Salvner, p. 107.

Chapter 5

1. Maryann N. Weidt, interview with Gary Paulsen, in *Children's Literature Review*, Vol. 19 (Detroit: Gale Research Inc., 1990), p. 167.

2. Gary Paulsen, *Woodsong* (New York: Bradbury Press, 1990), p. 9.

3. Gary Paulsen, *My Life in Dog Years*, illustrated by Ruth Wright Paulsen (New York: Delacorte Press, 1998), p. 2.

4. Gary Paulsen, *Winterdance: The Fine Madness of Running the Iditarod* (San Diego: A Harvest Book, Harcourt Brace & Company, 1994), p. 25.

5. Ibid., p. 24.

6. Ibid., p. 52.
7. Gary Paulsen, *Dogsong* (New York: Bradbury Press, 1985), pp. 79–80.

Chapter 6

1. Gary Paulsen, *Winterdance: The Fine Madness of Running the Iditarod* (San Diego: A Harvest Book, Harcourt Brace & Company, 1994), p. 94.
2. Ibid., p. 145.
3. Gary Paulsen, *My Life In Dog Years*, illustrated by Ruth Wright Paulsen (New York: Delacorte Press, 1998), p. 2.
4. Paulsen, *Winterdance*, p. 163.
5. Gary Paulsen, *Woodsong* (New York: Bradbury Press, 1990), p. 122.

Chapter 7

1. Jane E. Gardner, review of *Dancing Carl*, *School Library Journal*, May 1983, p. 84.
2. Dorcas Hand, review of *Dancing Carl*, *Horn Book Magazine*, August 1983, pp. 446–447.
3. Charlotte W. Draper, review of *Tracker*, *Horn Book Magazine*, June 1984, pp. 340–341.
4. Richard Luzer, review of *Dogsong*, *School Library Journal*, April 1985, p. 98.
5. *The Bulletin of the Center for Children's Books*, review of *Dogsong*, May 1985, p. 174.
6. Ethel R. Twichell, review of *Dogsong*, *Horn Book Magazine*, July/August 1985, pp. 456–457.

7. Gary Paulsen, *Guts: The True Stories Behind* Hatchet *and the Brian Books* (New York: Delacorte Press, 2001), pp. 19–20.

8. Gary Paulsen, *Hatchet* (New York: Bradbury Press, 1987), p. 125.

9. Zena Sutherland, review of *Hatchet*, *The Bulletin of the Center for Children's Books*, December 1987, p. 73.

10. Barbara Chatton, review of *Hatchet*, *School Library Journal*, December 1987, pp. 103–104.

11. Gary Paulsen, *Pilgrimage on a Steel Ride: A Memoir About Men and Motorcycles* (New York: Harcourt Brace & Company, 1997), p. 101.

12. Ibid., pp. 111–112.

13. Ibid., pp. 100–101.

14. Gary Paulsen, *Caught by the Sea: My Life on Boats* (New York, Delacorte Press, 2001), p. 79.

15. Ibid., p. 81.

16. Paulsen, *Pilgrimage on a Steel Ride*, p. 37.

Chapter 8

1. American Library Association, "YALSA: Margaret A. Edwards Award," 2000, retrieved January 1, 2002 (http://www.ala.org/yalsa/edwards/paulsen.html).

2. Betsy Hearne, review of *Nightjohn*, *The Bulletin of the Center for Children's Books*, February 1993, pp. 187–188.

3. Gerard J. Senick, ed., *Children's Literature Review*, Vol. 19 (Detroit: Gale Research Inc., 1990), p. 167.

4. Susan L. Rogers, review of *Nightjohn*, *School Library Journal*, March 1993, p. 223.

5. Rachel Bucholtz, "My Life's Work: Author," *Boy's Life*, December 1995, p. 28.

6. Nancy Vasilakis, review of *Woodsong*, *Horn Book Magazine*, November/December 1990, p. 762.

7. Gary M. Salvner, *Presenting Gary Paulsen*, Twayne's United States Author Series, Young Adult Authors (New York: Twayne Publishers, 1996), pp. 40–41.

8. Gary Paulsen, *Hatchet* (New York: Bradbury Press, 1987), p. 186.

9. David Gale, "The Maximum Expression of Being Human," *School Library Journal*, June 1997, p. 27.

10. Gary Paulsen, *Nightjohn* (New York: Delacorte Press, 1993), pp. 57–58.

11. Gale, p. 28.

12. Gary Paulsen, *Pilgrimage on a Steel Ride: A Memoir About Men and Motorcycles* (New York: Harcourt Brace & Company, 1997), pp. 177–78.

Index

Index

About the Author

Sarah L. Thomson is the author of *The Dragon's Son*, a retelling of the King Arthur legend for young adult readers, which received a starred review from *The Bulletin of the Center for Children's Books*. She has also written *Stars and Stripes: The Story of the American Flag*. After graduating from Oberlin College in Oberlin, Ohio, she moved to New York City to become an editor of children's books. She now works full-time as a writer and lives in Brooklyn with her two cats, who help with her writing by lying on the piece of paper she needs the most.

Photo Credits

Cover, p. 2 © Tim Keating.

Series Design and Layout

Tahara Hasan

Editor

Annie Sommers